Dear Parent,

In Why Do Birds Sing? your child will learn that birds sing to "talk" to each other. Wise Mrs. Owl tells Christopher that each song has a different meaning. Then she introduces Christopher to many birds, who sing him their special songs. How many you recognize? Turn the sten to the chirping

Sincerely,

Managing Editor

FAMILY FUN

- Set up a bird feeder in your yard. Help your child place b̶ ̶ ̶ ̶ the f̶ ̶ ̶ each da̶ ̶ As ̶ ̶ ̶ ̶ ̶ ̶ to le̶ with your chi̶ ̶ to the songs they sing.

- Visit the aviary at your local zoo or visit a pet store with your child. Listen to the many different bird songs.

READ MORE ABOUT IT

- *Why Do Birds Fly South?*

This book is a presentation of Weekly Reader
Books. Weekly Reader Books offers book
clubs for children from preschool through high
school. For further information write to:
WEEKLY READER BOOKS, 4343 Equity Drive,
Columbus, Ohio 43228

This edition is published by arrangement
with Checkerboard Press.

Weekly Reader is a federally registered trademark
of Field Publications.

Why Do Birds Sing?

A **Just Ask**™ Book

Hi, my name is Christopher!

by Chris Arvetis
and Carole Palmer

illustrated by
Vernon McKissack

FIELD PUBLICATIONS
MIDDLETOWN, CT.

You did –
and it's a bird!
Lots of birds sing.

Well, I am a bird.
When I sing, you hear
"Hoot, hoot!"
There are many kinds
of song birds.
Each kind has its
own song.

Hoot!

I hear you!

From morning to night, birds can be heard singing.

A bird talks to other birds with its song.

In early spring, the male bird sings to find a mate.

Once a mate is found, the bird sings more songs as it builds a nest.

Then the bird uses warning calls to keep other birds away from the nesting place.

When the baby birds are born, they use calls to get attention.

The peeping and chirping noises let mother bird know they are hungry or frightened.

The robin is one of the best song birds.
It sings a lovely good morning call and a different one for good night.
Robins sing best just before it rains.
The male robin sings a beautiful love song to talk to its mate.

He has a great voice !

Some sparrows and whippoorwills sing best at night.
The house wren sings a happy song all day long.

Some birds have calls that say their name.

The Blue Jay says, "Jay, Jay!"

The Chickadee chirps, "Chick-A-Dee-Dee!"

The Bobwhite calls, "Bob-White!"

The Cuckoo says, "Cuckoo, Cuckoo!"

The Mockingbird is very talented.

It can sound like any bird.

It can also cry like a cat or croak like a frog.

It mocks or *imitates* any sound it has heard.

Unbelievable!

Birds sing warning calls. The sharp "Caw" of the Crow lets other birds know of danger.

Birds call to each other when they want to get together.

These songs are called gathering calls.

You can hear gathering calls in the fall when birds get ready to fly south.

The honking geese and quacking ducks make loud gathering calls.

Quack!

Baby birds chirp for attention.
Loud calls give warnings.
Birds give calls to get together.
The birds sing to find mates
and build nests.
The bird songs fill the air
with music!

I love those sounds !